Pilgrim Places Holy Lives

A Gospel Journey With The English Saints

CHURCH HOUSE PUBLISHING

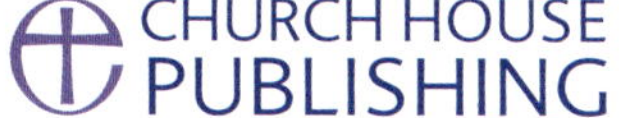

Church House Publishing
Church House
27 Great Smith Street
London SW1P 3AZ

www.chpublishing.co.uk

Published 2026 by Church House Publishing

ISBN 978-1-78140-555-0 (Single Copy)
ISBN 978-1-78140-556-7 (10-Pack)

Photo p. 8 from the British Library Collection: Yates Thompson MS 26 f.2r
Photo p. 20 from the British Library Collection: Cotton Nero D. IV, f.26v

EU GPSR Authorised Representative

LOGOS EUROPE, 9 rue Nicolas Poussin, 17000, LA ROCHELLE, France
E-mail: Contact@logoseurope.eu

Booklet design by penguinboy.net

Printed and bound in England by Core Publications Ltd, Kettering

Contents

Introduction

Each of us has our own story, but we are also part of bigger stories.

The greatest story ever told is that of God becoming human in Jesus to offer us a transforming relationship with him. In this devotional booklet, we will see how this amazing story took root in Anglo-Saxon England, and how those who responded to it became signposts to God. They not only changed the world around them but can still challenge, inspire, and encourage us today.

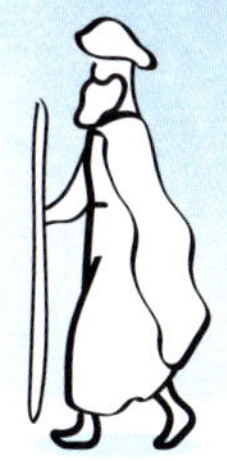

This booklet is designed to help individuals pray and reflect on the ancient practice of pilgrimage, inviting them on a spiritual journey with the early English saints. Through Bible readings, reflections, questions and prayers, this booklet invites us to reflect what it means to live as pilgrims on a purposeful journey through life.

Over the course of twenty-four days, each week focuses on two saints who helped to welcome the Gospel, dedicated their lives to God, and shared the Gospel with others. The saints are not merely a set of remarkable people from the past but fellow travellers on our pilgrim journey who continue to shape our identity, our worship, and our witness to the world.

May this journey with the saints strengthen our faith, deepen our understanding, and inspire us to play our part in the great Gospel story with renewed conviction and joy.

Archbishops Sarah Mullally & Stephen Cottrell

About the Contributors

Dee Dyas is the Director of the Centre for the Study of Christianity and Culture, University of York, and Heritage and Storytelling Lead for Faith in the North.

Sarah Mullally is the Archbishop of Canterbury.

Stephen Cottrell is the Archbishop of York.

James Shelton is the Director of the Cuthbert Centre for Pilgrimage and Prayer.

Sally Welch is the Vicar of the Benefice of Kington St Mary with Huntington, Old Radnor, Kinnerton and Titley in the Diocese of Hereford.

Jenny Wright is a Canon of Ely Cathedral.

Sammi Tooze is the Discipleship Adviser to the Archbishop of York.

Alexandra Zhirnova is the former Everyday Faith Editor.

A map of Pilgrim Places from this booklet

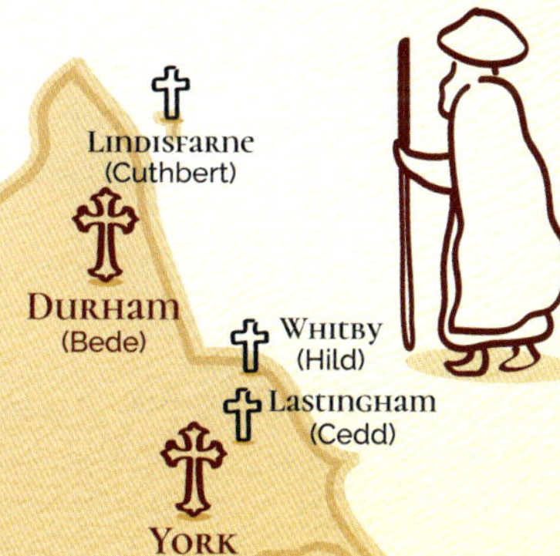

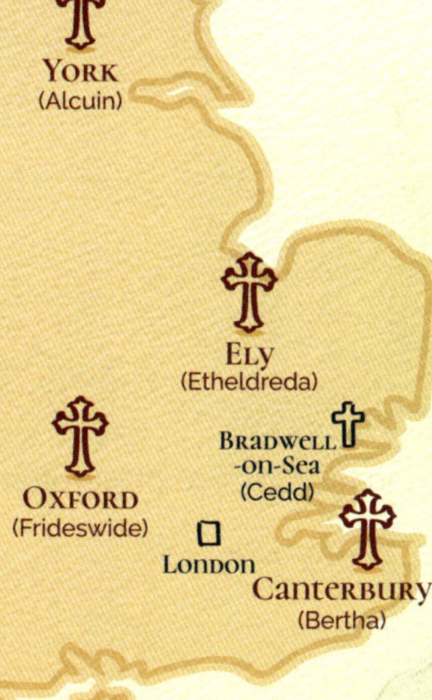

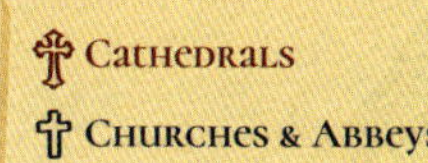

Welcoming the Gospel

This week, we explore how the Gospel took root in Anglo-Saxon England through the lives of St Bertha of Kent and the Venerable Bede.

Bede's writings preserve the story of England's Christian beginnings and remind us that the Church is always on pilgrimage, helping us to see God at work in every encounter with the Gospel, in every community, and every pilgrim journey.

We then turn to the story of St Bertha, who stands at the beginning of English Christianity. Bertha helped rebuild Christian life in Kent, welcomed the first Christian mission, and planted seeds of faith that transformed whole kingdoms. Together, their stories invite us to rediscover what it means to rebuild, to welcome others, and to see our lives as a great journey towards God.

A seated scribe (believed to be Bede) writing.
British Library Archive/Bridgeman Images.

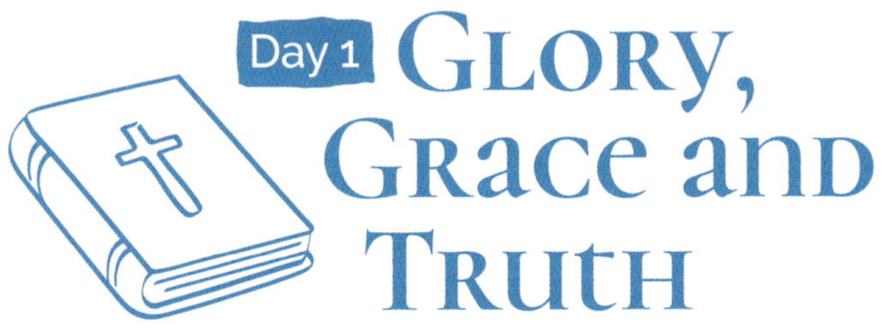

Day 1 GLORY, GRACE AND TRUTH

READ John 1.1-5, 10-14

In the beginning was the Word, and the Word was with God, and the Word was God.

The opening of John's Gospel tells the story of God made man, the Word made flesh entering human society, light coming into darkness and overcoming resistance. It is a narrative of glory, grace, and truth. It is a story of first-century Palestine. It also became the story of Anglo-Saxon England, with multiple mission initiatives bringing the Good News of salvation and transformation as the Northumbrian monk Bede (d. 735), whose feast day falls on 25 May, showed vividly in his *Ecclesiastical History of the English People*.

Bede, whose tomb is in Durham Cathedral, saw the planting of the Church in his own day as a dynamic continuation of the Gospels and Acts. Every conversion, miracle, and holy life demonstrated God at work in what Bede called the 'uttermost edge of the world,' just as the Bible showed God acting in Judaea, Asia, Greece, and Rome. God's Church, as Augustine of Hippo noted, was on a pilgrim journey through time and space, offering light and grace to all.

Mission, then as now, was neither easy nor straightforward. Yet the openness and courage of those who responded to and shared the Good News changed the world around them, enabling millions of us to follow in their footsteps through the centuries.

How excited are you about the Good News of forgiveness and new life?

Lord of life, may your Good News fill me with joy and wonder. Help me see how to share this amazing message with others so they too can know your love and light. Amen.

Day 2 PILGRIMS THROUGH LIFE

READ 1 Peter 2.9-11

Once you were not a people, but now you are God's people ... Beloved, I urge you as aliens and exiles [strangers and pilgrims] to abstain from the desires of the flesh that wage war against the soul.

In his writings, Bede introduces us to many 'saints': people whose lives were transformed by the Good News. At the heart of their response lay the conviction that Jesus Christ offered an eternal relationship and deep security which could not be found anywhere else.

Daily life in Anglo-Saxon England was full of uncertainty. No one knew when bereavement, a pandemic, war, or exile might leave them facing life alone. Change was a constant feature of a society shaped by migration and cultural influences from all over the known world. Against this background, Anglo-Saxon Christians saw themselves as pilgrims on a journey through life towards their eternal home. Recognising that nothing on earth will last for ever, they chose to invest in something more permanent.

As citizens of heaven, they had new values, and their security in God gave them the courage to take risks and make sacrifices to transform their world. The Gospel message of forgiveness and new life was urgently preached to rich and poor alike. Kings, queens, and other leaders were taught to use their power for good; laws and society were re-shaped to reflect principles of justice and care for others.

Responding to the Gospel means letting God transform our lives to reflect his love and values. What does God want to change in us and through us?

Lord of hope and transformation, help me to find my security in you and invest in what will last. May my daily journey through life reflect your mercy, grace and values as I serve you in your world. Amen.

Day 3 Inner Journeys, Special Places

READ Psalm 27.4-5

**One thing have I asked of the Lord
and that alone I seek: that I may dwell
in the house of the Lord all the days of my life,
To behold the fair beauty of the Lord
and to seek his will in his temple.**

As part of embracing the Good News, Anglo-Saxon Christians explored the spiritual benefits of both 'inner pilgrimage' and pilgrimage to special places to find forgiveness, healing, and new understanding of God. Each of these was seen as supporting and enhancing the longer pilgrim-journey towards heaven in a particular way.

Bede himself entered a monastery at an early age, withdrawing from the wider world to focus on an inner journey of prayer and learning about God. Within the framework of the daily pattern of monastic worship, Bede worked tirelessly to study God's Word and his world and to use his gifts to inform and enrich others. 'It has always been my delight to learn or to teach or to write,' he declared, and he prayed for, wrote to, and supported many others in their own callings, inside and outside the monastery.

Bede tells us that many people visited places in England, such as the shrines of St Etheldreda or St Cuthbert, to seek forgiveness or healing. Surprising numbers also went on pilgrimage to Rome in search of spiritual understanding and blessings, as well as resources to enrich the life and worship of the Church back home.

How do you resource your daily journey with God? Do you take time to pray, to learn, to experience his grace, truth and glory?

Dear God, as I journey through life with you, please help me to take time to listen to you and learn from you. Please walk with me and guide me every day. Amen.

Day 4

Rebuilding

 Isaiah 58.11-12

Your ancient ruins shall be rebuilt; you shall raise up the foundations of many generations; you shall be called the repairer of the breach, the restorer of streets to live in.

The story of Christianity became the story of Anglo-Saxon England with the arrival of St Bertha in 580.

St Bertha arrived in Kent as the bride of King Æthelberht – a young Christian princess from a foreign land. Christianity had first been brought to Britain by the Romans, but centuries of upheaval left its buildings ruined and its practices forgotten. Into this landscape of new customs and half-remembered faith, God led Bertha – not as a conqueror or a public reformer, but as a woman of prayer whose faithfulness prepared the Anglo-Saxon kingdom of Kent to welcome the Gospel.

Bertha's marriage was on the condition that she would be allowed to practice her religion. King Æthelberht granted her the old Roman church of St Martin on the edge of Canterbury. It was worn, neglected, and in need of care. Yet Bertha, with her chaplain Liudhard, restored and prayed in it daily. Long before St Augustine arrived to preach the faith in England, she was already rebuilding, making space for God's presence to be known again.

Her story echoes Isaiah's promise: God guides his people so that they may restore what has been broken. Bertha's example reminds us that rebuilding begins in small, hidden acts of faith: tending a place of prayer, renewing a neglected practice, choosing hope where others see ruins.

What 'ruined' or neglected place is God asking you to reclaim for prayer today?

God of restoration, guide us as you guided Bertha. Help us to repair what is broken, renew what has been neglected, and trust that even small acts of faith can become the beginning of new life. Amen.

Day 5

Welcoming the Stranger

1 Corinthians 3.7-9

The one who plants and the one who waters have a common purpose … For we are God's servants, working together; you are God's field, God's building.

Bertha's presence in Kent changed the course of English Christianity. When she became the Queen of Kent, Pope Gregory I wrote to encourage her to share her faith with her husband and restore Christianity to England. But Bertha could not do this on her own. Eventually, the Pope sent a mission led by St Augustine, knowing that Bertha would welcome them.

Because of Bertha's influence, King Æthelberht listened respectfully to Augustine's message. As Bede later recorded, the king sat outdoors to hear the

Gospel, while Bertha quietly prayed nearby. In time, the king was baptised, thousands followed, and the foundations of Canterbury Cathedral were laid.

Welcoming help from others can challenge our comfort and assumptions. But welcoming those who come alongside us is not a sign of weakness or failure, it is a reminder that God weaves his work through a whole community of people. He never intended us to carry every responsibility alone. When others step in with gifts we do not have, we are still valued, still called, still held in his purpose. Their presence is simply another way God shows his care for us and continues the work he has already begun.

Who might God be inviting you to welcome or support today? Or how might God be calling you to accept encouragement and help from someone else?

Lord of hospitality, open our hearts to those you send to walk alongside us. Teach us to receive them with grace, knowing that you created us to work together for your purposes. Amen.

Day 6
Planting the Seeds

READ Galatians 6.9-10

So let us not grow weary in doing what is right, for we will reap at harvest-time, if we do not give up.

St Bertha never saw the full extent of the fruit her life would bear. Yet the seeds she planted by bringing the Gospel to England continued to grow long after her death. What began in her small restored chapel on the outskirts of Canterbury would grow to shape the life of an entire nation.

Her daughter Æthelburh, raised in the Christian faith nurtured at Canterbury, married King Edwin of Northumbria and carried the Gospel with her into his kingdom. Like her mother, she asked for a chapel and brought a bishop to guide and teach. Like her mother, she lived a life of steadfast prayer, which ultimately helped lead Edwin and his people to Christ.

From Bertha's prayers in Kent would grow the great flowering of Christianity in the North: the faith of Hild at Whitby, the holiness of Cuthbert on Lindisfarne, the learning of Bede at Jarrow. She did not see the harvest, but she trusted the God who gives the growth.

Bertha's life encourages us to be patient sowers in God's kingdom. Many of our most faithful actions will bear fruit we may never witness. Yet God sees every seed of our faith, kindness, and hope, and uses them in ways beyond our sight.

When you are discouraged by lack of 'results' in your faith, how can Bertha's example inspire you to keep praying?

Lord of the harvest, help me to sow faithfully and patiently. Give me courage to trust that you will bring fruit in your time, and that every seed planted in love has a place in your story. Amen.

Living for the Gospel

This week, we journey with two remarkable saints whose lives continue to shape the story of Christian faith. St Cedd and St Cuthbert lived in an age of movement, mission, and deep dependence on God.

Their ministries grew from places of prayer and community, yet both were marked by a willingness to step beyond the familiar for the sake of the Gospel.

Cedd's story reminds us that every Christian community is meant to be a place of learning and sending. His work of healing division and communicating across cultures offers wisdom for our own fractured world. Later in the week, Cuthbert's example draws us into a deeper awareness of prayer, humility, and the quiet faithfulness that enables a life of service.

These reflections invite you not just to admire the saints of the past, but to join them – seeking God's call, listening for his voice, and stepping forward in faith.

A 'carpet page' depicting an elaborate cross from the Lindisfarne Gospels. British Library Archive/Bridgeman Images.

Day 1 BEING Sent

READ John 15.5-6

Jesus said to his disciples, 'Those who abide in me and I in them bear much fruit.'

While visiting Holy Island in Northumbria a few years ago, it dawned on me that what for us, today, is a place of arrival, a holy place we come to on pilgrimage, was, for those who established it, a place of departure. The monastery that Aidan founded there in 635 was a place where people were formed in the Christian faith in order to be sent out to live and share that faith with others.

One of these people was Cedd. He was born around 620. He became a monk on Lindisfarne along with his brothers. In the year 653, he sailed down the east coast of England and landed in Essex at a place now called Bradwell-on-Sea – also a beautiful place of pilgrimage – and established a monastery there. Cedd was part of a missionary movement that spread from Northumbria to Essex and then, Cedd's final resting place, up to Yorkshire, where he established another monastery in Lastingham, where others were formed in the Christian faith and then sent out.

Cedd teaches us that every Christian church should be a school for disciples, a place where people learn the way of Jesus together and are then sent out to share his love with others. And though we treasure the physical buildings of our churches, the boundaries of this mission, which began with Jesus calling those first fishermen, run through human hearts and are led by the Spirit. When we visit the sacred places associated with these Anglo-Saxon saints, we should arrive in the same spirit as those who came to Jesus: ready to be sent out.

Where might God be calling you that requires you to step out in faith? What are you being asked to leave behind?

Loving God, I thank you for those who have taught me the way of Christ. Deepen my commitment to worship and prayer so that when I read the scriptures, I can hear your voice speaking to me, know your love for me and even be able to share that love with others. Amen.

Day 2 HEALING DIVISIONS

There was a great multitude that no one could count, from every nation, from all tribes and peoples and languages ... before the Lamb.

Cedd was one of the translators at the Council of Whitby in 664. This was a momentous event in English church history. The emerging Anglo-Saxon church, which owed much to both Roman and Irish Christianity, now had to choose which of these traditions should prevail. Although the presenting issues don't seem of huge significance to us now, the real issue was about authority and unity, and this is important. You cannot serve two masters, says Jesus. A house divided against itself will fall.

As the Christian faith spread and developed in England, so it became important that it lived united under one authority and there was a powerful argument that this should be the one that was shared more widely across the rest of Europe. Cedd himself was probably on the Irish side of the argument, the side that eventually lost. But whatever his own views, his role in the process was as a kind of broker between the two positions, enabling both sides to hear each other clearly. This is a remarkable ministry. It is much needed today. How can we translate the unchanging message of Jesus Christ into the ever-changing cultures and languages of the world? And in a church made up of so many different languages and cultures itself, how can we hear each other?

Why not take the trouble this week to listen to someone whose perspectives are different from your own? Ask them for their views and hear how their questions can help us understand our own faith better.

Generous God, help me to see you in others and to learn from the example of others. May your unchanging Gospel be translated into the ever changing languages and cultures of the world. And help me to remember that I still have much to learn. Amen.

Day 3 · A Gospel Community

Jesus said to Simon, 'Do not be afraid; from now on you will be catching people.' When they had brought their boats to shore, they left everything and followed him.

St Cedd's primary vocation, like ours, was to know and follow Jesus. His mission, what it meant for him to be sent out by Jesus, was as to share the Gospel and to plant churches. And for Cedd, as it should be for the church today, those two things belong together: to bring people to Jesus is also to bring them to his Church. The Christian life is to be lived out in a community of mutual love and service. The Church is the body of Christ, where no one can do it alone. It reflects and shares in the very life of God who is a community of persons: Father, Son and Holy Spirit. That's why planting churches and establishing new Christian communities is one of the best ways to show the message of Christ, the joy of the Gospel, and the difference it makes to human life. It was through these Christian communities that Cedd proclaimed the Gospel and many came to faith.

Even his death has a certain relevance for us today, since he and many of the monks at Lastingham died of the plague in 664, as a vicious pandemic swept the country. We too have recently lived through a pandemic. We saw many people suffer and die. We have all become a bit more aware of our frailty and our mortality. Cedd shows us not only missionary zeal in life, but faithfulness in death. He knew that the good things he received from Jesus and shared with so many others were just a foretaste of the glory to come.

Look for an opportunity this week to share your faith with someone else, or even just an aspect of your faith. Show how it sustains and inspires the way you live your life each day.

Gracious God, open to me a door of opportunity that I can share something of the gospel of Jesus Christ with someone somewhere today. Use me for the building of your Kingdom here on earth. Amen.

Day 4
Co-builders in God's Kingdom

READ 1 Corinthians 3.10-12

According to the grace of God given to me, like a skilled master builder I laid a foundation, and someone else is building on it. Each builder must choose with care how to build on it. For no one can lay any foundation other than the one that has been laid; that foundation is Jesus Christ.

Yesterday, we prayed to become builders of God's kingdom. Today, our reading encourages us to see that we are all working together, incorporated into this common purpose across places and ages. It is a purpose more majestic than anything we could ever imagine by ourselves. The very fact we are reflecting on the lives of these saints helps to make this point. We are drawing inspiration from individual lives, lived in service to Jesus and stitched together for a greater purpose. These are disciples through whom the Good

News was spread throughout these lands. For the rest of this week, we remember a saint who dedicated his life to building God's kingdom on earth: St Cuthbert. Cuthbert and Cedd's lives are closely connected, as both owe their calling to St Aidan, who first brought the gospel to Northern England. First, in his teenage years, Cuthbert was given a supernatural vision of Aidan's soul ascending. This was a pivotal moment of commitment, when Cuthbert decided to become a monk. Later, he would become Prior and then Bishop at Lindisfarne, the monastery founded by ... Aidan, who laid the foundation on which Cedd and Cuthbert built. Whilst we may never fully grasp the scale of God's kingdom building during our own lives, our individual contributions can be worked together to achieve incredible things for good. As followers of Jesus, we are co-builders in God's kingdom. What a vision for a life!

Jesus invites you to come, follow him and become a co-builder in his kingdom. What could that look like for you today?

Holy Spirit, please help us notice and understand the gifts we have been given and the contributions you call us to make. Amen.

Day 5 CALLED AND CHOSEN

READ 1 Samuel 16.6-13

But the Lord said to Samuel, ' … The Lord does not see as mortals see; they look on the outward appearance, but the Lord looks on the heart.'

All are called to believe and follow, though the Bible also teaches that some are chosen by God to fulfil specific purposes. In today's reading, Samuel, the great Prophet and last Judge of Israel, meets Jesse and his sons to anoint the future King of Israel. To even Samuel's surprise, God's choice isn't the obvious. David, the youngest, hasn't even been brought for consideration. Yet it is he who God chooses for the task.

While the young Cuthbert was, like David, familiar with tending sheep, his life didn't reflect kingly privileges, and he actively chose to forego things as part of his witness. For example, at a time when bishops dressed like princes and had servants, Cuthbert continued to live like a monk. Because of his humble appearance, many thought he was unsuitable to be a leader, but God chose him for his heart, not his looks. Today, people often feel under pressure to meet the expectations of others. Cuthbert's example is of a person whose identity and worth were found in God's love, not the validation of others. I am convinced that Cuthbert lived with an enduring sense of mystery as to why he had been chosen to receive such profound experiences of encounter and provision. However, Cuthbert's humility meant he would never have thought himself as being special. With the benefit of time, it is clear that Cuthbert was chosen to fulfil specific purposes. And this was because God saw that he could grow the seed of faith in Cuthbert's heart.

Our human inclination is to look to outward appearances, yet the Bible teaches that God looks to the heart. Try to look past something you dislike about yourself or someone else today, too.

Father God, thank you that you look to the heart. Help us to interpret our experiences in life as ways to grow our dependence on you. And please use us in the fulfilment of your great redeeming purposes. Amen.

Day 6 Rooted in Love

READ Ephesians 3.16-19

I pray that ... Christ may dwell in your hearts through faith, as you are being rooted and grounded in love. I pray that you may have the power to comprehend, with all the saints, what is the breadth and length and height and depth, and to know the love of Christ that surpasses knowledge ...

Cuthbert's ministry was marked by the way in which he oscillated between two places: the monastery, where he prayed, and the road, where he preached. Cuthbert is remembered and celebrated for his work amongst the poor, where he shared the Gospel and performed miraculous acts in Jesus' name. But his life was rooted in a reliance on God's love and power through prayer. In other words, private prayer is what sustained his public ministry. I love the story of Cuthbert going out into the wild surroundings of Lindisfarne to pray alone through the night.

When I think of Cuthbert withdrawing in this way, I can't help but feel that today's reading, taken from Paul's letter to the Ephesians, would have been in his heart. For it was in prayer that Cuthbert came to grasp the full breadth and length, height and depth of God's love. This is a humbling realisation for anyone, and it is the place from which we, like Cuthbert, are meant to move. It is telling that, as Cuthbert's fame grew, his desire to seek solitude in prayer only increased. When he was invited to become a Bishop, Cuthbert initially refused. Eventually, he was convinced to take up the role. But I wonder how many people could honestly say that, like Cuthbert, they would prefer greater intimacy with God in prayer over an opportunity to increase in human standing and power?

If prayer is the place where our inner lives are grown, do we make enough space for it? Consider your prayer life and how you might like to develop this over the coming year.

Jesus, thank you for your unconditional love and amazing grace. Help us to open ourselves to receive these gifts and make them the cornerstone of our identity, in which everything else is found. Amen.

Trusting the Gospel

This week, we follow the journeys of two holy women whose lives show how trust in God can fill our lives with hope. St Frideswide, the patron saint of Oxford, and St Etheldreda, the patron saint of Ely, discovered their vocations early in life but had to wait many years before their calling was fulfilled.

Their lives were shaped by moments of fear, long stretches of waiting, and the quiet routines of daily service. Yet in each of these places, Frideswide and Etheldreda discovered that God was present – always at work in ways often hidden from view. Their faith and patience help us remember the promises of the gospel and renew our trust in God's plan for our lives.

Ely's Norman Cathedral, built on the site of the Abbey founded by St Etheldreda in 673. Church of England/Timothy Selvage.

Day 1 TRUSTING WHEN IN FEAR

READ Luke 8.22-25

They went to him and woke him up, shouting, 'Master, Master, we are perishing!' And he woke up and rebuked the wind and the raging waves; they ceased, and there was a calm. He said to them, 'Where is your faith?'

In the Latin Chapel of Christ Church Cathedral, Oxford, is a vast and colourful stained-glass window. Designed by Edward Burne-Jones in the late nineteenth century, it tells the story of St Frideswide. St Frideswide was an eighth-century Saxon princess who established the religious community which was the forerunner of modern-day Christ Church – unique in that it is both a college of Oxford University and the cathedral for the city of Oxford. Before St Frideswide became a nun, she was pursued by a king, called Algar, who wanted to marry her. The stained glass depicts her fleeing the city and being forced to hide.

One of the most striking scenes is of the saint hiding in a pigsty from Algar. Bright-pink pigs form a wall around her as she clings to a wooden pillar, asking for God's help to hide her. So too might we, in times of anxiety, fear or even danger, direct our heartfelt prayers towards the God who always hears us, and always answers our prayers.

Sometimes, the answers are a long time coming. Sometimes they are answered in ways we do not expect, but no prayer is wasted. 'Trust in God,' the Bible tells us, again and again, reassuring us that in our journey through life we are never alone.

Spend some time remembering an occasion when you were aware of God's presence with you. You might want to write or draw how this made you feel, to remember for future times.

Mighty God, give me the courage to put my trust in you. When I reach out in the darkness, let me feel your hand take mine, so that I may walk safely until I am once more in the light. Amen.

Day 2 TRUSTING WHILE WAITING

READ Romans 15.5-6, 13

May the God of hope fill you with all joy and peace in believing, so that you may abound in hope by the power of the Holy Spirit.

About three miles from Christ Church Cathedral and the city of Oxford, at the end of a narrow, tree-lined track, is the church of St Margaret of Antioch, Binsey. According to legend, St Frideswide stayed here after her escape. She was probably here for three years, until she felt safe to return home. The well in the churchyard is dedicated to St Frideswide, and there is evidence that it became a 'retreat house' for the community she founded. The saint herself is said to have spent time there in prayer and reflection.

After the terror of capture and the adrenaline rush of escape, St Frideswide might well have felt relieved to find herself in such a small, out of the way place, with occupations very different to those of a princess. Perhaps she felt frustration as well, as time went on and nothing much appeared to be happening.

We all have seasons in our lives when everything appears to be 'on hold' or we need to be in a place or carrying out a role which is necessary but not ideal. Our prayers might appear to be unanswered. Our purpose in life undefined or unfulfilled. These times can be challenging but we should not despair, for God is present in the waiting. During these times we can hold fast to the promises of God. We can trust that beneath the dark earth of today there lies hidden the green shoot of tomorrow, offering hope and new life to each one of us.

Reflect on some of the 'green shoots' in your life – the early beginnings of adventures in spirit, mind or body? How might you nurture them?

Eternal God, your existence is beyond time and space. Give me patience and hope in the waiting times, so that I might trust in your good purposes for my life. Amen.

Day 3 Trusting in the Everyday

Love is patient; love is kind; love is not envious or boastful or arrogant or rude. It does not insist on its own way; it is not irritable or resentful; it does not rejoice in wrongdoing, but rejoices in the truth. It bears all things, believes all things, hopes all things, endures all things.

In the same part of the Cathedral as the glorious Burne-Jones window, there is another image of St Frideswide. The colours are not as bright as the larger stained glass, for it is five hundred years older. In this image we see St Frideswide as the founder and leader of a religious community. She has no small responsibility, and her rich, red cloak and heavy gold crown reflect the practical and spiritual authority she held. Her slender figure appears almost too slight to bear such weight. But her face is calm and wise as she gazes solemnly upon the cathedral's many visitors.

How many hours must she have worked, dealing with the daily administrative tasks of running a community! And how careful must she have been always to be mindful of God's presence, to listen for his wisdom and to trust in his word even in the midst of the busyness!

Today's world is fast-paced and hectic. It is easy to lose sight of God amongst the noise and clamour of everyday life. But we can't let Love – the patient living – out of our faith through our interactions with each other and our world – be drowned out by selfishness and greed that try to overwhelm us. We may not always manage the habit of daily prayer and reflection which is the heart of religious life. But we can look out for God's presence among the everyday actions which make up our daily lives.

What sort of structure is your faith built upon? What regular habits sustain it? How might you build in extra support?

Everyday God, help me to be faithful in the small things as well as in the great, so that I might increase my trust in you and fill my days with your praise. Amen.

Day 4 JOYFUL in Hope

READ Romans 12.9-18

Do not lag in zeal, be ardent in spirit, serve the Lord. Rejoice in hope, be patient in suffering, persevere in prayer.

There are many sayings and proverbs we could quote to remember that good things come to those who wait; but waiting is a difficult place to be. Many of God's most faithful disciples spent a long time waiting for something. Paul urges the Church in Rome to not lag in zeal, to be ardent in spirit, and to serve the Lord. A hearty pep talk if ever there was one! Married twice, Etheldreda had to wait twelve years before her yearning to join a convent came to fruition. While we don't know much about her life, it seems that her hope in her calling remained firm. She didn't waver from a life that was lived in service of Christ, despite being princess, wife and queen before becoming nun and abbess. Her patience and steadfastness led to her founding the

Abbey in Ely, the foundations of which have nurtured and sustained a Christian community for centuries.

This place of prayer has cared for the sick and offered hospitality to the stranger over many hundreds of years. There has been almost continually a community that rejoices and weeps, that prays and seeks peace. It can be difficult to drown out the noise of the world that doesn't promote this kind of communal being-together. But we need to hold firm to our hope. We are called to persevere and to hear God's voice above all the other distractions. Faith asks us to trust that even if today is not the day in which our plan comes to fruition, God is at work in our lives; our hope will be fulfilled.

It can be difficult to be patient, particularly when we have been waiting a long time. Where do you need to cultivate hope and perseverance in your life?

Faithful God, help me to love more generously, serve more graciously and seek your peace always. Keep my attention on you that I may see with your eyes, and cling to the hope that is found in you. Amen.

Day 5 Renew Our Strength

READ Isaiah 40.27-31

Those who wait for the Lord shall renew their strength, they shall mount up with wings like eagles, they shall run and not be weary, they shall walk and not faint.

One of the stories about Etheldreda's life tells the tale of her fleeing from Northumbria and finding shelter with her sisters under a miraculous ash tree. The ash tree grew from her staff planted in the ground. It is easy to be anxious about having what we need, both physical resources as well as our own skills.

It is easy to question God's calling – are we equipped? Do we have the right education and talents? Do we know the right people? What if we find ourselves strangers in an inhospitable country? And yet, throughout Scripture and the history of the Church we encounter ordinary people doing extraordinary things, because they trust God and they are filled with the Holy Spirit. It is God who is at work, not us. And that is why we remember, too, that we do all things for the glory of God, not for our own glory or vanity. Our work is always in the service of the Kingdom of God. Just as Etheldreda miraculously produced the shelter that she and her companions needed, so too do we need to hold fast to God's promise that if we hope in the Lord, we will renew our strength. That which seems impossible for us is possible with God.

Our task is to learn to hear God's voice amid the noise of daily life so that we can discern where it is that we are being called and trust that God is already there.

Overcoming imposter syndrome can be difficult. Where do you need to trust God more, knowing that God will give you everything you need to do God's work?

Generous God, still my anxious thoughts. Pour out your Spirit upon me, that your power might strengthen and sustain me always, and daily I might trust you more; through Jesus Christ our Lord. Amen.

Day 6
THANKSGIVING

READ Philippians 4.4-9

Do not worry about anything, but in everything by prayer and supplication with thanksgiving let your requests be made known to God. And the peace of God, which surpasses all understanding, will guard your hearts and your minds in Christ Jesus.

It is impossible not to worry, because there is always something to worry about! But worrying often doesn't do very much to change things. What changes things is how we speak about our worries and how we act; in short, our attitude does much to determine what happens next.

When Etheldreda became a nun, she still had a lot to worry about. Her community was swept by a deadly epidemic, and Etheldreda herself eventually fell ill. Yet we know that even during this time of distress, the saint continued her work, praying, caring for her nuns, and giving thanks to God. It is easy to be distracted by all that is going on in our lives, our families, our communities and the world. But we need to stay focused on what we have been called to do and who we are. While God's peace will not make all that is anxiety-inducing disappear, it can help us to look at what is important. Worry can shrink our world, making us bitter and angry. Being joyful and giving thanks for what we have can help us to find God's peace, always. Paul reminds us that this peace is only found in Christ Jesus and that is what we need to focus on. God's faithfulness is demonstrated again and again in Scripture, in the lives of the saints and everyday stories. We need to cultivate this trust in our lives, so that when the time comes, we are ready to answer God's call.

How can you better cultivate an attitude that rejoices always and gives thanks to God, especially if you are worried or anxious about something?

God of peace, quiet my heart and mind, that I may be reasonable and gentle in word and deed, through Jesus Christ our Lord. Amen.

Light of the Gospel

This week invites us to explore how God's light shines on us through learning, reflection, beauty, and community.

St Alcuin of York, whose life spanned both scholarship and deep pastoral care, shows us that wisdom is not merely an academic pursuit but a way of walking closely with God. His letters reveal a man shaped by Scripture, attentive to the struggles of his age, and unafraid to name the darkness he saw around him. And yet, even in times of grief and uncertainty, Alcuin held fast to the truth that God's light is never overcome.

As the week continues, we turn to **St Hild of Whitby**, whose story shines with the steady radiance of hope. Her life reflects how God's light can take root in difficult times, illuminate the future, and kindle gifts in others. Hild and Alcuin remind us that light multiplies when shared.

The ruins of Whitby Abbey. St Hild became its founding abbess in 657.
Photo by Quan-You Zhang on Unsplash.

Day 1 WALKING IN DARKNESS

READ Psalm 139.10-11

**Even darkness is no darkness with you;
the night is as clear as the day;
darkness and light to you are both alike.**

Alcuin was born around the year 735, somewhere near York. He had quite a remarkable life, beginning in the cathedral school of York where he was taught by Aelbert, himself a student of Bede. Later in life, Alcuin became Master of the school, and was so well-regarded that the Emperor of the Franks, Charlemagne, invited him to Aachen to be Master of the Palace School. In both these places, Alcuin's love of learning nurtured many in his time and years to follow.

But Alcuin also lived through times of great distress. We still have two letters he wrote which reveal to us the devastation Alcuin felt when Vikings attacked the monastery on Lindisfarne in 793. In his letter to the Bishop of Lindisfarne, Higbald, Alcuin writes, 'the distress of your suffering fills me daily with deep grief ... Heathens destroyed the house of our hope.' I'm sure that many of us will have experienced moments like this in our lives, where darkness feels like it is pressing in, and the light becomes more difficult to find. In our reading today, we are reminded that God is just as present in the darkness as in the light – that to God, the darkness and light are both alike.

The Bible often shows us that God's deepest work happens in times of uncertainty, waiting, and struggle. In our own shadows, we too are invited to pause, to breathe, and to discover that God is already with us. As Alcuin writes later in his letter to the Bishop of Lindisfarne, 'God never deserts those who hope in him.'

When darkness presses in and hope feels fragile, pause and trust that God is already present, quietly at work in hope and love.

Eternal light, to whom the darkness and light are both alike, shine into our hearts, that we may learn to seek you in all places, and walk in your ways. Amen.

AFTER ALCUIN OF YORK (804)

Day 2 Illuminate Our Path

READ Psalm 119.105

**Your word is a lantern to my feet
and a light upon my path.**

Alcuin was devoted to his own learning, as well as being a teacher and educator. He understood that Scripture could offer wisdom and steadiness in times of fear or sorrow, as well as those of joy. In his work as a scholar and teacher, he encouraged others to engage with Scripture as something to shape everyday life as we encounter God, not just something to study. It shaped his thinking, steadied his faith, and helped him respond with care to those around him.

In Psalm 119, we read, 'Your word is a lantern to my feet and a light upon my path.' For Alcuin, the Bible was just that – a light in the darkness, showing the way when uncertainty pressed in. It guided him not only in study but in the whole of life, offering comfort when grief or distress threatened to overwhelm him. Through its stories, prayers, and teachings, he learned to see both the challenges and joys of each day in the light of God's love and presence.

We too are invited to let the Bible illuminate our path and form us in faith. By reading, reflecting, and carrying its words with us in everyday life, we can find direction in our choices, courage in difficulty, and wisdom in ordinary moments. Like Alcuin, we discover that God's light is often quietly at work, and doesn't just shine in extraordinary times – it walks with us every step of the way.

When might you pause to read a passage or a story from the Bible today, and how could its wisdom help you bring light, courage, or hope into ordinary moments?

Eternal wisdom, scatter the darkness of our ignorance, and by the light of your word teach us how to live and guide us in the paths of love. Amen.

AFTER ALCUIN OF YORK (804)

Day 3 THE BEAUTY OF HOLINESS

**O worship the Lord in the beauty of holiness;
let the whole earth tremble before him.**

Have you ever walked into a building and simply stood
in awe at its architecture, its colours, stone, or glass?
Our world is full of impressive buildings, many of them
built centuries ago with limited technology. Each was
carefully designed, and in the case of churches, crafted
with faith and theology so that the buildings themselves
tell us something of God's story.

Alcuin played a key role in shaping the spiritual vision of
Aachen Cathedral. As a trusted advisor to Charlemagne,
he guided not only the teaching and worship within
the palace school, but also the design of the church
itself, ensuring that it reflected the story of God and the
life of the Christian community. His influence helped
the building become more than stone and glass – it
became a place where learning, prayer, and worship

met, where architecture itself could lift hearts and minds toward God.

All our churches are places of encounter, worship, hospitality, welcome, and fellowship. Our churches point beyond themselves, beyond the beauty of stone to the beauty of holiness. In almost every church, whether grounded in simplicity or bursting with grandeur, it is possible to walk around as a pilgrimage, encountering something of God's story in stained glass, in crafted ceilings, in baptismal fonts, and in the invitation to gather around God's table where all are welcome. In our churches, we can pause to let the spaces, the light, and the imagination in which they have been created quietly draw us into a deeper encounter with God.

Where in your church, or in the places you pass each day, might you pause to notice the beauty, imagination, or holiness around you?

Eternal goodness, shine into the places we gather; give us wisdom to see the beauty of your holiness, that with all our heart, mind, and strength we may seek your face all our days. Amen.

AFTER ALCUIN OF YORK (804)

Day 4 Light for the Future

READ Isaiah 9.2

The people who walked in darkness have seen a great light; those who lived in a land of deep darkness – on them light has shined.

St Hild, who founded Whitby Abbey, was born into a time of uncertainty and violence. In the seventh century, Northumbria was a fractured landscape of kingdoms at war – a 'land of deep darkness'. Hild's own father died when she was a baby, poisoned by his enemies. For Hild's mother Breguswith, who had a small child and was pregnant, this must have been the darkest time of her life. And yet God gave her hope of a brighter future.

One day, Hild's mother dreamed that she was searching for her husband and could not find him. When all her hope was gone, she noticed a precious necklace under her clothes. And this necklace was shining so brightly that it lit up all of Britain. The Venerable Bede, who wrote down the story of Hild's life, tells us that this dream was not just a mother's hope. It was God's promise of the future generation carrying his light into a broken world.

We don't need to be told that we, too, live in a 'land of darkness'. We see it wherever we look around. But today's reading reminds us that darkness does not have the last word. God sent us his Son to be our light, and continues to send people to guide us towards this light. Like Breguswith's necklace, hope is always within reach.

**What signs of hope can you see,
even in places that feel dark or uncertain?**

Loving God, through your Son Jesus Christ your light has shone into the world. As we journey through life with you, may we not despair over the power of darkness, but look towards the light with hopeful hearts. Amen.

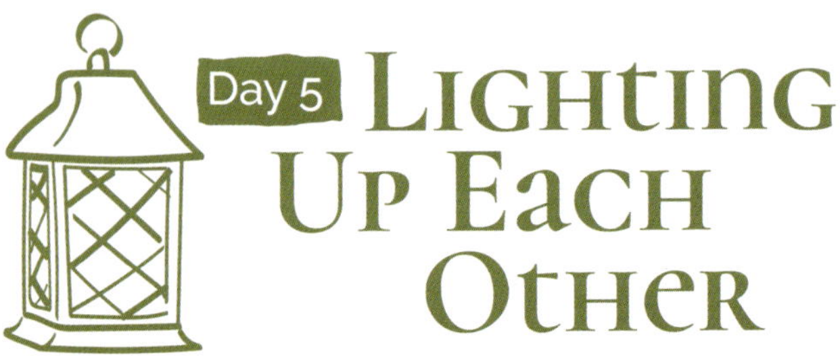

Day 5 LIGHTING UP EACH OTHER

READ 1 Thessalonians 5.11

Therefore encourage one another and build up each other, as indeed you are doing.

In the Anglo-Saxon age, many Christians believed that that God might call them to travel as pilgrims and to serve him in unfamiliar places. This was true of many of the saints we read about, like Cedd, Cuthbert and Alcuin.

When Hild reached her mid-thirties, she too wanted to find a new way to serve God. She left her home and community, planning to go across the sea to become a nun in Gaul. But before she left England, her bishop begged her to stay and help him build a new monastery.

The monastery which Hild founded at Whitby became a beacon of faith and learning. Perhaps the most important person nurtured in Hild's monastery was Caedmon, the earliest English poet whose name we know. Caedmon was not an educated man: his whole life he had been a cowherd. But then, one night, an angel appeared to him, giving him the gift of poetry. When Caedmon came to Whitby, Hild did not turn him away but encouraged him to join the community and dedicate his life to writing poems of praise to God. None of this would have been possible if Hild had gone abroad as she wanted.

Many of us want to meet God in special places. But time, money, people who depend on us, or physical limitations often stand in the way. If this is where you are, do not despair. Know that, just like Hild, God might have a purpose for you where you are.

Whose light has guided you recently – and how might you become a source of light for someone else?

God, give us eyes to see your light shining in other people. Help us to encourage it, not extinguish it, and give us wisdom to lift each other up. Amen.

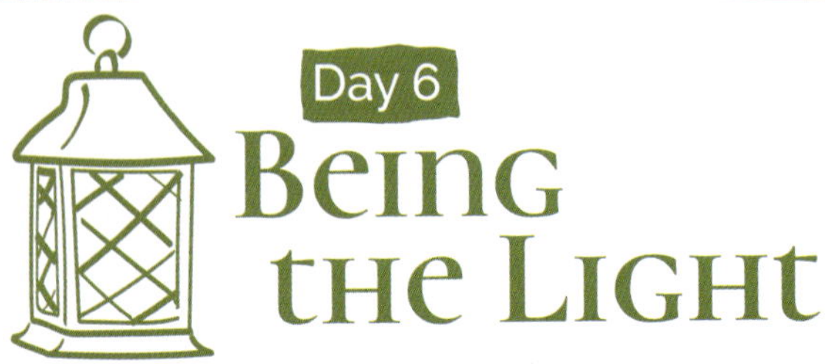

Day 6
Being the Light

 Matthew 5.16

Jesus said, 'Let your light shine before others, so that they may see your good works and give glory to your Father in heaven.'

Have you ever met someone that made you think: 'I wish I was more like them'? Or maybe it's someone whom you never met in person – but who changed your life nonetheless?

For medieval Christians, this is exactly what saints were: people so filled with divine light that it overspilled into the lives of others, even when the saints were long gone. According to Bede, Hild 'was not only an example of holy life to members of her own community, but also brought about the salvation of many living far away, who heard the inspiring story of her hard work and goodness.'

Hild's story embodies the truth in today's reading and shows what it means to lead a holy life. Formed by faith through years of steady discipleship, Hild became someone whose wisdom, integrity, and care illuminated the lives of others. Kings sought her counsel; ordinary people called her 'mother' for her grace and love; and generations after her death continue to be inspired by the story of her faithfulness. The same is true for all the saints in these reflections: each in their own way, they carried the light of the Gospel.

We may not lead abbeys or advise kings, but God still invites us to become bearers of his light, wherever we go each day. Like Hild, we can choose a way of life shaped by prayer, generosity, and sharing the Gospel. And as we do, Christ's light, shining through our ordinary actions, may become a source of hope for those around us.

Look for one opportunity today to bring Christ's light into an ordinary moment: through kindness, wisdom, or courage.

Lord of light, help us to walk faithfully with you on this pilgrim journey and make us beacons of hope for others. Amen.

GOING FURTHER

Where will your pilgrim journey take you next?

We hope that you have enjoyed *Pilgrim Places, Holy Lives*. Here are some possible next steps for your journey:

- Connect with God all year round with the Everyday Faith app. Follow daily reflections like those in this booklet to inspire, equip and encourage you in your everyday faith. The app is free to download for iOS and Android via **cofe.io/EverydayFaithApp**

- Find further resources to engage with pilgrimage via **cofe.io/Pilgrimage**

- Explore the stories of those whose beliefs and actions helped create the landscape and society we live in today via **faithinthenorth.org**

- Explore the **Pilgrim** range of discipleship resources for individuals and groups, including '*The Pilgrim Way: A Short Guide to the Christian Faith*' via **pilgrimcourse.org**

- Discover thousands of services and events, groups and activities taking place at churches near you and online all year round via **AChurchNearYou.com**